MUSINGS
from ME

STEHANIE J. BARDY

DARK MYTH
www.darkmythpublications.com

Dark Myth Publications, a division of
The JayZoMon/Dark Myth Company, LLC.
21050 Little Beaver Rd, Apple Valley, CA 92308

ISBN: 978-1-7372947-9-5

First Printing May 2022

Dark Myth Publications is a registered trademark of The JayZoMon/Dark Myth Company, LLC.

10 9 8 7 6 5 4 3 2 1

Other works by Stephanie J. Bardy:

- **The World of Myth Anthology Volume IV** – *Penance* – Dark Myth Publications
- **Natural Instincts Tales of Witches and Warlocks** – *Word Witch* – Zombie Works Publications
- **The Chosen** – Dark Myth Publications
- **Full Moon & Howlin: A Werewolf Anthology** – *Pack Business* – Zombie Works Publications
- **Monsterthology 2** – *Salla* – Zombie Works Publications
- **The World of Myth Anthology Volume III** – *The Huntress* – Dark Myth Publications
- **Eternally Bound** – Dark Myth Publications
- **A Pagan Testament** - Brendan Myers

This is dedicated to all those who have supported not just my writing, but my poetry.
To my Dad, who left way to soon.
To my Poppa, who told me I WAS an artist, that I painted with words.
To Dana Rondeau, my Muse on more than one occasion. I miss you Butterfly.
And to the boy with the smile, who took a chance on a girl with a book.

Table of Contents

Table of Contents (Cont'd)

Table of Contents (Cont'd)

Table of Contents (Cont'd)

Introduction

When I sat down to do the introduction to this book, I was preparing to do a podcast. I had no idea what to say about this eclectic collection of poetry. It has no rhyme, no reason, and no definitive theme.

I was stalling.

Then I thought about what this book represented to me. It has so many of my thoughts, my fears, my joy, and my anger woven into the well-crafted, carefully chosen words. It is many years of pain, sorrow, and growth.

Poems that saw me through my first breakdown, my last child, and all the growth in between; It had inspired me and given me an outlet when my heart was in so many pieces I wasn't sure if I would ever find them all. Poetry has allowed me to be silly and serious, raging, quiet, and helped me explore emotions I couldn't give an outside voice to.

While there isn't a set theme other than an alphabetic one, there is a very good, very deep look into my life, who I started as, who I struggled with, and who I am now.

The poems will take you to places I don't ever want to go again, and some I never want to leave. They will have you laughing and dancing or thinking deeply about moments in your own life.

Today, I am a woman with a strong sense of who she is, most of the time. I have made friends with my demons, sat and had tea with them, and danced in shadows with them. I have mourned the loss of loved ones, my Dad, my Poppa, and my friend Dana. I have said a Silent Goodbye to another friend, stood in the rain, and cried.

I started writing poetry as a way to escape the emotions I wasn't equipped to deal with. It came easy to me, and while they may not all be works of poetic art, they are real.

My process is a strange one. The poem just appears in my head, and I get this frantic, almost panicked feeling welling up inside of me. I will scramble almost blindly for anything to write on and to write with.

Many of my poems, once written down, are gone from my head. Like it was someone else's words flowing from my hands. I go back later and read them and have this strange feeling of not having written it at all. I know I did; it's my chicken scratch on the paper.

I hope you find something you can connect to; many have over the years. I hope you find a poem you relate to or understand in some way.

Welcome to the alphabetic chaos that is the emotional roller coaster that I ride. It is rough, it is funny, it is angry, and it is sad. You may experience highs and lows, as with any roller coaster, and your face may even get wet, hopefully with tears of laughter. But, like all rides, it is worth the price of admission.

Stephanie J. Bardy
April 26, 2022
Ontario, Canada

MUSINGS *from* ME

A PARENT'S CRY

Little ones, rest your soul.
Wrap it safe inside my heart.
Lay your cares upon the wind.
Release your fears and let them part.

Little ones, your eyes to close.
Beautiful windows, to you inside.
Save your worries for another day.
Let sleep take you on a magical ride.

Little ones, in gentle repose.
Face so soft, so free of fear.
In body though I may not be seen.
Know my heart and feel it near.

Stephanie J. Bardy

A PROMISE

The wind blew a promise by my face today.
As the rain came dripping on down.
It tickled my cheeks and tousled my hair.
Then blew the promise all over town.

It whispered to trees, and to bulbs still long buried.
Of sun, and of shine, and of days yet to come.
And the rain kept on falling all over the ground.
Sending ribbons of hope to the gutters to run.

The blanket of white, she pulled back so gently.
With glimpses of much warmer days.
It stirred the birds singing off to search for a mate.
With whispers of Springtime, and the warm summer haze.

The wind brought a promise, I know she will keep.
To bring a dazzling color array.
Tree's bursting with beauty, and grass oh so green.
If we sit and wait patiently, just one more day.

ALWAYS REMEMBER

I always remember
>The house in Pickering where I learned to read
>And played with the dogs
>I was up to your knee
I remember Christmas's there and my big coloring book.

I always remember
>Those long hot bike rides down Balmer road in the dust and
>blazing sun
>But the ride was a must
>At the end of that ride was you, with a hug
When I want to remember, its those memories that tug.

I always remember
>The dock on that day
>And my glee and excitement
>Because you were on your way
>The happiness I felt before I went in the drink
Kept me close to the surface, you didn't let me sink.

I always remember
>Those rides in the car
>From school to Toronto, it wasn't that far
>But "She drives me crazy" on the radio did play
And it still makes me smile to this very day

I always remember just not always out loud
For you are my Auntie, and for that I am proud
You loved and you hugged me scolded me some
But I always remember, and those memories come
The role Auntie holds more than one word should allow.
And mu love for you keeps growing some how
If you ever feel lonely and so far from your own

Stephanie J. Bardy

Always remember my heart is your home.

AND YOU WERE REAL

My mind, my heart,
Race to that one moment.
A lifetime ago, it seems
When I touched your face,
And you were real.
When I held your hand.
And you were real.
You touched places
I had long forgotten
Opened places
Long since closed.
I became real
I became human
You breathed me into existence
And you were real.

Stephanie J. Bardy

AWAKENINGS

Ancient whispers echo,
in the fading light.

A wild spirit awakens,
to chase the restless night.

Amber eyes trail,
the darting of a deer.

The beat of the dark,
is all she can hear.

A lone cry shatters her calm,
like that first rushing wind before the raging storm.

AWARENESS

Trapped inside my head
Words fly out
Making no sense of the nonsense
That is the sense of my world

Stephanie J. Bardy

BLUE MOON INSPIRATION

Silver streaks cross my windowpane.
Breaking the darkness of my tomb so very still.

Restless heart beats like the animal trapped within.
Silent screams crack my lips, spreading my mouth wide.

The darkness presses close, like an old friend.
Yet those silver streaks still cross my windowpane.

BREATH OF FALL

The rain races down the abandon streets
On this sacred Sabbat night.
The Elements mark the change of the season
With thunder crashing might.
Lightening flashes, and the wind does roar
Pounding the earth with their might.
Summer has ended and Fall rings in.
As he claims this time as his right.
The trees hold on valiantly to their leaves
Desperately with all of their might
But none is so strong as the Breath of the Fall
On this Autumn Equinox night.

Stephanie J. Bardy

BROKEN

Pieces of my life
Lie scattered at my feet.
Trust. Hope. Faith.
Glisten in the rawness of the morning sun.
Love. Peace. Joy.
Tiny pieces. So delicate. So fragile.
One word tore them from me.
One sentence.
One moment.
Threw them about and laid them bare.
Can I pick up the shards?
Will they stab?
Will they cut open the wounds to place them back?
Piece by piece.
Recreating what was.
Broken.

BUTTERFLY FLY
Dedicated to Dana R.

She stands.
On the farthest precipice of the highest mountain, she has ever had to climb.
Her arms are stretched, head raised gently to the warmth of the sun.
At her back she feels the comfort, the whispered cushion of the world of love behind her.
 Heart racing, body shaking, she lifts one tiny foot and steps forward.
Steps into the unknown, with a smile, and the faith of one who knows.
 And she flies. She soars on wings painted with all the colors of the rainbow.
Higher and higher, shining brighter than the sun.
Lifted, guided, and held up by those she will remember.
And by those who will never forget.

Stephanie J. Bardy

CASTLES AND CARS

Struggle.
Its what we do.
Who we are.
They say it shapes our character.
We all struggle.
Rich and poor alike.
The rich just do it in style.
I don't wish for riches.
To have more money than needed.
For I would lose my creativity.
 I wonder if the Rich have ever taken a camp chair to the moon.
Or raced a Kleenex box to the finish line in the Indy 500.
 Can they look in their cupboard?
And create a meal out of gravy seasoning, rice, and soup.
Can they laughed until their sides split, sitting under a leaky tarp?
I'm sure they can, but can they appreciate the wonder of it?
 I do not wish for more than I need, because I can create all that I
want.
Turn that box into a castle fit for any Queen. Create a meal out of
almost nothing,
And have my family asking for more.
And win the Indy 500 and have a tissue to wipe the tears.
 I can sit under that leaky tarp, and revel in the joy of close friends.
For I do not believe that it is money that makes us happy.
Sure, it makes us comfortable, but not happy.
It is the love of friends, sisters, brothers, family.
Even in the midst of true heart ache, unbearable pain,
and the never-ending bills, we know.

We have each other. Even when we fight, deep inside,
down in that place only a few can see. We know.

We will always have each other.

CLICK

The phone clicks and you are gone.
Back into the ether, back into what I pray is not a dream.
A million miles away, your smile remains,
And a million miles away, my heart longs to feel that heat.
Click the phone connects and one more time I hear that voice.
That smooth velvet that slips down my subconscious into places
That remain in dreams.
Click.
That is the sound of my life as it starts and stop.
Click and you are gone.

Stephanie J. Bardy

COILED

Pressure builds
Like a tiger coiled in my chest.
I can feel the claws
Trying to burst out.
Breath, step, breath, step.
Walk away they say.
Walk away.
Easy, if I didn't want to scream.
Easy if I didn't want to smash the face
of the ignorant gaping hole screaming at me.
The tiger paces within me.
I will not let it out.
Breath, step, breath, step.
I will not let it out.

COME TO ME

Come to me on gossamer wings
Brilliant light glowing in the black cloak of night
Dust my eyes
Enchant my heart
Dripping nectar between my lips
Come to me on gossamer wings
To dance around the fire bright
Lighten my step
Guide my hand
Within the forest deep
Come to me on gossamer wings
Within your realm
Within your keep
Lost in the fairy way

Stephanie J. Bardy

CREATURES OF THE MIST

Mist slowly caress's the green hills.
Darkening in the twilight.
Slowly the magic of the night awakens and stretches her arms wide.
Darkness, deeper than life,
Raises his head and howls.
This is his time.
 Hunger gnaws at him,
And he must answer the call.
They must all answer the call.
These creatures of the dark.
Creatures of the Mist.
The ethereal cover provides a cloak,
Over the eyes of the innocent.
And they move through it as one.
They have a great love for their prey.
For they are what gives them life.
And they must live.
They must survive.

To have balance we must have both.
The wonders of the light, and the darkness of the night.
 The Creatures of the Mist.

DARKNESS FALLS

Darkness falls
And the veil has thinned
Calling the dead
And letting them in
Release our pain
To let them cross
Know in your heart
They'll never be lost

Stephanie J. Bardy

DAWN

Light stretches her tired fingers towards my window.
Dawn steals the Nights thunder, rendering him powerless.
She comes on padded feet, gentle and serene.
He fights her, like a warrior, harsh, abrupt, and vengeful.
Opening her arms wide she embraces all.
He is defeated and crawls back into the shadows.
Another day is born.

DELICATE DEALINGS

Hearts are fragile, when loved behind its walls.
Battle worn and scarred, mended with stitches that tell a lifetime of tales.
Hearts can be beaten, broken, bruised, and shattered.
And then, burst with a love so strong it makes you weep.

Hearts can be hidden, tucked away for safe keeping.
Guarded like a precious jewel, or a delicate flower.

Hearts are never fair trade, when dealing with delicate matters.
They are a prize hard won, freely given, and recklessly abandoned.

Hearts can be taken for granted or granted for the taking.
But they can never be given back.

So tiny a thing, really, no bigger than a fist.
And yet, in matters of emotion, it is bigger than the world.

Unconditional, unconventional, and completely unpredictable.
Breaking, bending, loving without reason, or fear.

The many wounds, cuts and nicks, that weave that lifelong tapestry.
Wouldn't, couldn't, shouldn't ever be replaced.

My heart keeps beating, keeps loving, keeps breaking.
Each story it tells, speaks of a bounty of riches.

It is mine for the caring, mine for the giving, and here for the loving.
And I wouldn't trade it for the world.

Stephanie J. Bardy

DIRT
Part One

I smell dirt
Dark. Rich
The kind that leaves the taste of blood on your tongue.

The kind that signals Life as it claws its way through the decay of the
Fall.
Forcing itself through the flesh of the Mother.

I smell dirt.

The kind that gets under your nails, streaks your cheeks and stains
your knees.
That smell after a good rain, or a patch that has been freshly turned.
The kind that clings to your senses, picking at that primal part of you.

I smell dirt.
It is floating on the inky blackness of my yard.
It is gently stroking the tender branches of the majestic trees that
stand guard.

I smell dirt.
I hear life.
I am alive.

DIRT
Part Two

I smell dirt.

That plunge your hands into it, plant your seeds, caked under your nails, and stain your knee's kind of dirt.

That smell that reaches into the core of your primal and runs wild, and barefoot through the green and the dark.
Where your very being touches every leaf, every hoof, every stone.
The raise your arms at the thunder, and laugh at the lightening, kind of smell.

I smell dirt.
That rich, full of life, full of promise, full of retribution, smell.
That raging storm a-coming, pounding rain, puddles forming kind of smell.
Where only the wild things live, the dark things dance, and the cycle of life begins and ends.

I smell dirt.

Stephanie J. Bardy

DISENGAGE

I fear I must disengage myself for a while.
I have stepped below the water line, where my head likes to bob, just above the surface.
The stairs, cold on my feet, only go down, in that long endless spiral.
Worry not my darlings, for I have many someone's, somethings, who greet me with their sneer's, and their laughter. If I turn the right way, it's almost joyous. Ringing pure in the sheer facade of familiarity.
The tears are hot, scalding even, tracing rivers of memories down my cheeks.
They bring warmth into this cold, cold heart.
Do not be sad, for it is but a journey, an adventure of sorts, full of peril, and swashbuckling, and a pirate, who steals my breath.
I am but a moment away, miles if you count, a blink.
I fear I must disengage myself for a while.

DRUM CIRCLE

Tribal breath fueled by the primal heat.
Ancient rhythm carried by the vessels chosen.
Sun drenched bodies illuminated by the flames of the fire.
Voicing the melody of the Mother.

Stephanie J. Bardy

DRY LEAVES AND BRITTLE BONES

Dry bones clatter and the cold wind blows.
Leaves, dried and brittle, skitter across the toe of my shoe.
It is a time for death, a time for dying.
A time for those who have gone before
To walk among those that remain.
The dark time is upon us, but if we stop,
Be still, and listen,
The love of those who have gone before
Will whisper through the branches of the fast-asleep tree.
Life will pulse and dance in the breath of the cold,
And the promise of dry bones and brittle leaves
Will warm us until Spring

EARTH, AIR, FIRE, WATER

Rain drips from my lips
Poised inches from sure destruction
Fire becomes liquid in my veins
My breath stolen in one look
Solid ground meets my feet as the embrace ends.

Stephanie J. Bardy

FALSE PRETENSES

Pity, shrouded in the pretense of acceptance.
False smiles, hollow laughs.
Truth prevails, with the setting of the sun.
Evil revels in the dark, ice tinkles ominously.
Stomachs clench in fear.
Who is the subject of the fury tonight?
Who will succumb to the devil with the southern drawl?

FAMILY

I stand, in the shadows, and I listen.
Birds call in mating, the tree's sigh softly, and the distant sound of laughter.
I watch from my secret place, as the motley crew of my life play their parts.
My heart smiles, for beyond the wood and windows, is love immeasurable, acceptance unconditional, and people who are oh so dear.
 Young and old, each holds a piece of who I am.
The intricate weaving of the tapestry of family.
My family.
As my face feels the warmth of the sun, my spirit feels the bond unbreakable, the commitment unshakable, and with joyful step, I take my place within.

Stephanie J. Bardy

FIELD OF FORGOTTEN PROMISES

Sun dappled skin
Caressed by the dark hand of fate
Needing the promise of warmth
Limbs entwined in a battle of senses
Both pushing for control
Midnight and Morning
Meet in the drenched darkness of a well-lit
Field of Forgotten Promises

FOR THOSE WHO CAME BEFORE US
Dedicated to my Poppa, Harry Benjamin Austin. RCAF

Become a random act of kindness,
Be thankful that you can.
For those who went before us,
Are the ones who gave a damn.

With a coffee, hand, or smile,
Pay it forward if you choose.
For those who went before us
Had everything to lose.

Share a moment with a Vet,
With their plates all Poppy red,
For the ones who went before us
Not enough is ever said.

For the ones who went before us,
Gave their life without a pause.
For Freedom in our Country
Fighting someone else's cause.

Keep vigil in your heart,
Each day of every year
For the ones who went before us
And the ones who still are here.

Stephanie J. Bardy

FOR WE ARE WOMEN

I stood in the rain, and I cried today.
I wept and I keened for a soul that has been swept away.
I wailed and I whimpered for those left broken behind.

I let the drops carry my tears to the earth at my feet.
I let the thunder carry my voice to the sky.
I let the lightening brighten my heart.

I stood in the rain, and I cried today.
For beauty that I had the privilege to see.
The power of the storm matched the ache in my heart.

But I stood in the rain, and I smiled today.
As my pain washed away in the stream.
My feet gripped the Earth, and my face felt the sky.

For we are women, and we are strong.
We will dance in the moonlight.
And see the sun rise tomorrow.

FOREVER AND A DAY

The wind dances through your hair
You gaze out over the water
The wind dances through my hair
I gaze out over the water

So much the same, yet so far.

Close your eyes and I am beside you
Close my eyes and I feel your breath on my cheek
Open your arms
I will be there
Open my heart
Your already there

When you sleep
Feel me beside you
When I dream
Feel you inside me

When you wake
Know I love you
When I wake
I know you love me

Miles apart
Body and touch
So close inside
Heart and soul

You are my love
My light
The air that I breath
You are a thought

Stephanie J. Bardy

A tear on my cheek
Hearts joined as one
Beating in time
With the sound
Of Forever and a Day

FOREVER IS A MYTH

Look into my eyes and tell me what you see.
Look into your heart, is there room enough for me?
Take my hand and we'll fight these dragons together.
You can take my heart, but I won't promise you forever.
I can touch your face and that's real enough for me.
The smile on your lips is all I need to see.
Forever is a myth.
All we have is a moment.

FURY UNLEASHED

Rage, self-contained.
Burning just below the surface.
Liquid to his lips,
Stokes the fire within.
Anger claws forth.
Choose a target.
Aim, fire, destruction.
Self-loathing, propelled to another.
Empty glass refilled once more.
Comfort in the fiery liquid.
Embraced like an old friend.
Fury unleashed at the bottom of a bottle.

GILDED CAGE

Trapped inside a gilded cage of broken boards and cracked windows.
Dreams soar above my head, just beyond my fingertips, like ripe
berries, for my hungry soul.
Keys to the cage held by a shadow who dances in the dark of my
secrets.
Doors open and yet I set inside that cage, to afraid to see beyond my
own insecurities.
Trapped inside a gilded cage of my own making.

Stephanie J. Bardy

HAUNTED

Bodies come in the dark.
Broken thoughts.
Fragmented words.
I waken, and they are gone.
Back into the shadows.
So, I drift off again.
And they return.
Words I don't know.
Names I have never heard.
They haunt me.
In the night.
Only when I sleep.
Only when I dream

HE IS DRAGON

Scales fall, littering the ground.
Talon's reach, inches from me.
I tremble but stand firm.
Majestic and noble.
Wisdom of the ages in his eyes.
I am humbled before him.
I am honored to be in his presence.
I have intruded here.
In his cave, his sanctuary.
But he welcomes me.
He welcomes me.
I have no words.
No thoughts, just emotion.
He is Dragon.
To me he is home.

Stephanie J. Bardy

HEART SONG

Fragile times, our hearts have seen.
Strew upon the clover.
More ragged now, than its ever been.
In muted rumbling glory.

Each scar it bears, tells tales so true.
Of life most vigorously spent.
Reaching out, as hearts will do.
For love most joyously sent.

That one complete, that missing part.
Of puzzles deep and rare.
For a moments beauty, where miracles start.
With magic in which to share.

Fragile times, our hearts have seen.
With memories of clover.
The lines form now, where smiles have been.
The youthful time is over.

With age brings wisdom, to be passed on.
To keep the heart song going.
The secrets shared when we move on.
Will keep that love still flowing.

HEAVEN HELP

Heaven help the hand that closes. Sailing forth in an angry rush.
Heaven help the mind that closes.
Shutting out life's changing push.

Heaven help the silent children.
Forced to hide their pain away.
Heaven help when hearts are breaking.
Give them voice to have their say.

Life is not a game. From which you win or lose.
Life is a winding pathway.
Different ways for you to choose.

Open minds to hear the hard things. Open hearts to accept the truth.
Open hands to hold the crying.
Open arms with which to soothe.

Heaven help us all learn kindness.
Make our choices fair and true.
Heaven guide our steps of journey
Give us strength to see us through.

Heaven teach the child the wisdom
Of speaking from the heart
Heaven guide their precious footsteps
To the place from which to start.

With our ears we hear the words. But our hearts can feel the truth.
Listen softly, and with patience.
Never judge or disapprove.

Heavens guide the hand that opens.
In a gentle helping way.

Stephanie J. Bardy

Heavens guide those thoughts, erratic.
Help us find the words to say.

Heaven teach us all humility.
No one's better than the rest.
Heaven hold us in your arms.
Help us achieve our very best.

Musings From Me

HOPE

I am so very small, just a tiny little thing.
I live inside your heart, just waiting to take wing.
I have no special powers, or fancy names with which to call.
I'm not really thought of, not very much at all.

But when you pay attention, and you let me have my way.
Mountains can be moved, and inspiration comes to stay.

Call me what you will, hope, faith, or courage grand.
Just believe in who you are, and then just take a stand.
Impossible is possible, in every way you think.
For thoughts have more power, than any magick drink.

Listen to your voice, the one way down deep inside.
Don't let your fears take over, don't let your magic hide.
Faith is the strongest weapon, in doubt that takes a hold.
Belief in things so awesome, only you can be so bold.

So, listen, pay attention, and take my tiny hand.
And we can walk together, across this sacred land.

Stephanie J. Bardy

I AM A GROWN WOMAN

I am a Grown Woman
I have a Grown Woman's body, and a Grown Woman's face.
I work a Grown Woman's job, at a Grown Woman's pace.
I buy Grown Woman's clothes, and those sensible shoes.
I have Grown Woman's bills and have paid all my dues.
I have a Grown Woman's duties, to clean and to sup
I have Grown Woman's kids, and some have Grown Up.
I have Grown Woman's friends, and nights on the town.
Then laundry and dishes, and laws to lay down.
But inside there's a secret.
In this Grown Woman's heart.
A portion, a corner, a very small part.
Is still but a child, with a childlike care.
Who will still climb a tree, on a very good dare.
Who snuggles with blankets all safe and all tight.
When the monsters come calling on a dark stormy night.
She listens with glee, and with innocence rare.
And she bounces through days, with nary a care.
She lives deep inside, this Grown Woman's soul.
She lives there quiet peacefully and will never grow old.
She knows that the Woman, all contented and Grown
Will take care of the Child, of that she has shown.
When Grown Woman giggles, and runs through the leaves,
Or listens for hoof-prints above the house eaves,
It is Child who is playing, in Grown Woman's face,
And Child who can slow down, Grown Woman's pace.
The two are but one, in shape and in size.
Just look into Grown Woman, look in her eyes.
For though life's duties may wear her body down.
Child will come springing and soften that frown.
So, if you think you have lost, the Child within.
Take Grown Woman for a walk, in the newness of Spring.
Let her dance in the leaves on a crisp Autumn day.

Musings From Me

And Child will come peaking, and with you she'll stay

Stephanie J. Bardy

I AM A HOUSE PLANT

I am a house plant
With complicated emotions
I need sunlight and water
I need faces and voices
I need touch
I need to feel loved
And be love
I am a human house plant
And I am wilted

I AM DEATH

The crunch of leaves reminds me that life once dwelled in this barren land.
Vitality once flowed though the veins of the twisted roots beneath my feet.
Hope graced the branches above and the dirt below.
Helplessness skitters past my foot in the form of a dry brown leaf.
The silence weighs heavy on my shoulders.
I take a breath
I am done.
I am death.

I CHOOSE

I choose
I live in a world of my choosing, my creation. Every aspect of my life,
I have orchestrated to be exactly where I am.
I am in control and have control over myself and the world around
me. Every up, every down, every broken dream and shattered heart,
I planned. I chose to have because I knew it would take me here.
Nothing happens without the firm grip of my hand, my desire.
And yet, he is there.
Watching, waiting. He knows every move, every nuance, every
breath. He knows every step, every choice, claiming them.
I know he is there. I have seen him. In my dreams, dancing in the
shadows, moving about me, breath soft on my cheek. Always in the
shadows, always on the fringe, in the farthest reaches of my mind. He
lives in those places that I am too afraid to go. I have locked the doors,
but he holds all the keys.
He whispers to me, in my slumber. He laughs at my facade of
control.
I choose. I choose to ignore his existence, his being. I choose to turn
my back and with a wave of my hand, convince myself that I have
banished him from my world.
But those dark places, those edges of my conscious, he waits. Sitting
easily upon his throne made of my wishes, my hopes. He waits.
For he knows, complete control always breaks, always falls away into
chaos. He waits, for then, when all is lost, all is spinning wildly, he
knows, it will be his time to reign. His time to take control.

I'M HEARING VOICES
Inspired by the Beauty of the Mother, on the beach at FOTD
(story at the end of the song, explaining how it came into being)

I'm hearing voices, coming in from the waves.
I'm hearing voices, of long ancient days.
I'm hearing voices, their calling out to me.
I'm hearing voices, rolling in from the sea.

I'm feeling sadness, coming up from the ground.
I'm feeling sadness, in everything around.
I'm feeling sadness, as She washes away.
I'm feeling sadness, Mother's crying today.

(chorus)

Quiet voices for everyone to hear.
Quiet voices, from far and from near.
Mother's calling, she's crying out to me.
Mother's dying, it's time for everyone to see.

I'm smelling progress, its clogging up the air.
I'm smelling progress, ripping into homes so dear.
I'm smelling progress, eating all the trees.
I'm smelling progress, from the dying of the sea.

I'm seeing Chaos, smiling from a far.
I'm seeing Chaos, driving every single car.
I'm seeing Chaos, standing tall and proud.
I'm seeing Chaos, wrapping Mother in a shroud.

(chorus x2)

So, been going to FOTD for a few years. This was my 4th. I have
never made it down to the beach. This year, I made the trek, with

47

Dana and Char. We laughed and giggled our way down the drunken fun house stairs and emerged onto a beach with water as far as the eye could see. So many little treasures I had seen over the years brought back from the land, and there, in front of me, was the treasure, just waiting for me to discover.

We wandered down the beach, and found an old fallen tree, and we sat and enjoyed just being. As we sat and talked, we were blessed with a visit from a bald eagle. We watched her dip and soar as she taught the three smaller birds that followed her how to ride the thermals, swoop, and soar. Then she flew off, in search of dinner, I am sure. And we watched the three smaller birds play. Each jockeying for lead, diving towards the water, then soaring up into the sun. It was beautiful.

The sun started going down, so we decided to head back up. As we walked back down the beach, I could hear a faint tune in my head. The closer we got to the stairs, the louder it became. Then the words came. They fairly flew into my head, faster than I could keep up. I looked over at Dana, wide eyed. She asked what was up, so I told her, I had this song in my head, and I sang the first two stanza's. By the time we reached the top of the stairs, I had all 4 stanza's and the chorus.

And no paper.

Thankfully, I had a book in the van that I was reading, and it had pages at the end for notes.

And that is how this one came into being. I am very thankful, and humbled.

IN A DREAM I HAD

In a dream I had
The night was black as pitch
The wind beat a torrent on my doorstep
And howled down the flue

The moon a heavy lidded seductress
Beckoned me come forth
Out into the inky blackness
Down the path of stone

My feet found their footing
Carried me deep into the arms of the forest
They embraced me, closing out the world around
The soft whisper of water guiding me

The pristine waters lay before
With the moon winking up at me
"Look here my child" she said from above
"Look deep, beyond what your eyes can see"

The mirror cracked, giving way to time long past
Fairy lights danced in my hair, as it spiraled about my face
Visions fly faster than light
And he is there

Darker than night, he sends fear with a look
But I stand unafraid
For he is but a reflection of me
Emotions buried deep

I smiled, and winked at the moon
Hand widespread I shattered the image with a laugh
That which you know, can no longer harm

Stephanie J. Bardy

That which you face, becomes nothing

In a dream I had
The night was black as pitch.

IS THIS WHAT I WISHED FOR

Woke up this morning, head spinning with life's latest crisis.
I stumbled down into my kitchen for that first cup of liquid life.

As I desperately clung to my cup, I surveyed my empire.
The heart of my kingdom.

Scattered with remnants of breakfast.
Dryer sheets lounged lazily on the floor, snubbing their nose at me.
For having escaped, if only for a moment, their final fate of heat
register heaven.

I wandered into my living room.
All sad and faded looking in the pale morning light.
The laundry that had taken up residence in the chair, waved at me.
Looking for all it was worth, like it belonged.

My third or fourth hand couch, frayed at the corners.
Offered comfort for my desolate soul.

My kingdom? My empire? What I dreamed of as a little girl?
Is this it? Was my imagination so lacking that this is what I wished
for?

No. It wasn't. My empire, my very legacy wasn't in a faded carpet, or
cluttered surfaces.
It wasn't in the unfinished laundry, or the dirty dishes.

My immortality lay sleeping upstairs, it lay at school, struggling to
learn math, and it lay with a boy/man trying to make it on his own.

For in my childish dreams, in my girlhood fantasies, I had wished for
love.
I wished for a love that thought I was beautiful, before coffee.

Stephanie J. Bardy

Love that had patience when I was not.
Tolerant, when I was not.
Unwavering when I was not.

And I had found it.
In the dirty dishes from my daughter's breakfast.
In the dryer sheets from the load of laundry my husband did.
On the faded carpet, where my sons and I wrestled and laughed.
And on the desolate couch, where we curled as a family.

That is my Kingdom, my empire, my little piece of immortality.

LOOKING THROUGH THE FOREST
A Kid's Action Poem

Wrote this little poem for my nephews and granddaughter. It has lots of fun actions and gets them moving.

Looking through the forest, and what do I see? (hand over eyes, like your looking)

Two silver eyes looking back at me! (point to eyes)

"Run" said my brain (hands on head)

And my heart skipped a beat. (skip once in place)

"Run" said my brain

"Lets move those feet" (jog in place)

Looking through the forest, and what do I see? (hand over eyes, like your looking)

Long sharp teeth grinning back at me! (use fingers like fangs at mouth)

"Run" said my brain (hands on head)

And my heart skipped a beat. (skip once in place)

"Run" said my brain

"Lets move those feet" (jog in place)

Looking through the forest and what do I see? (hand over eyes, like your looking)

A gray wolf's face looking back at me! (hands around face)

So I stood very still, and I didn't make a sound. (stand very still, and no talking)

As the gray wolf sniffed the air all around (make sniffing sounds and actions like a wolf)

He turned his back, and slowly walked away. (turn around and walk slowly in place)

And I will remember him, each and every day! (clap the last part)

Stephanie J. Bardy

MARK MY WORDS

The lyrics of a song, and the tale of the fantastic life of a sister,
Made me wonder what my legacy would be.
Will I make my mark, and leave a space,
Or fade off into the shadows, a passing thought on a day full of
hearts?

What kind of memory do I want to be?
Do I want to be remembered for me?
Some grand tragedy, bemoaned, and wailed.

Then, words.
Words came to me, flowing into my head.
Bouncing around on all my uncertainties, tickling my insecurities.
And rapping sharply between my eyes.

When I'm gone my mark won't matter, my space won't be empty.
Life will continue, and the wheel will turn.
Children will grow, have children of their own, and I will become a
picture in a book.
Put away on a shelf.

The time is now, the space is here.
The mark I make are my words.
The love I share, with those I choose, the hands I hold with care.
They are my legacy, they are my place, they are what I will leave
behind.

Each moment I have, each breath that I take, is a journey,
On a road that only my feet can tread.
What I carry with me, is what matters now.
When I look in the mirror, and the Goddess looks back from my eyes,
When I start every battle , with the answer to what love would do,
I will create my legacy, and carve out my mark.

Musings From Me

The words that I write, the ones floating in my head,
Are my guides on the journey I take.
They tell my story, in pieces and bits.
The highs, the lows and the glory.

They say to live each day like you were dying,
But I say, Live each day like you were LIVING.
Live your life, by rules that make you work, creeds that make it hard.
Forgive when you can't, love when you won't,
Help when you need it the most.

For life is to short, to carry a grudge, and a chip belongs in a cookie.
Frowns cause you wrinkles, and hate makes you tired, and rage is the
tool of a rookie.
My words may not rhyme or always make sense,
But they are my own to leave behind.
I thank the Gods, for a gift so precious,
For the windows into my mind

Stephanie J. Bardy

MAY EVE

Faeries are dancing, with flickers of light.
As we welcome this fine May's Eve.

Bodies spiral and twirl, on the verge of flight.
Rejoicing in Winter's reprieve.

The Goddess brings life to the soil once more.
As we join in this Beltane Rite.

Drumming and singing, as witches of yore.
A-Maying we go on this night.

The trees are a-bud, and the flowers poke through.
In the warmth of the new coming season.

May is the month, for Spring is its due.
But Beltane's really the reason.

MOTHER, WARRIOR, GODDESS

I am Mother
From my womb life sprang forth
I nurtured life at my breast
And watched my children grow
Now I must fight
My children have ripped my womb from my very body
 And left gaping holes
My children have forgotten
The nurturing and the love
Which I had shown them
Now I must fight
Fight for my survival
For their survival
I will defend my children
Support my children
And die for my children
Or die because of my children
They spit on me
They bury me in the remnants of their excesses
They burn me
Gouge me
And betray me
Yet I still love them
I still nurture them
I still sustain them
I am Mother
I am Mother Earth

Stephanie J. Bardy

MYSTIC MOON

Back deck inspiration....the leaves haven't fully come in yet, so I can
still see the Moon through the branches...hence this was born.

Mystic Moon, Mystic Moon
I see you through the branches high.
With the Star's as your adornments,
I see you with my Spirit eye.

I see the passion in your face,
Though you seem cold to those so near,
I feel the warmth of your embrace
As you light my paths of fear.

Mystic Moon, Mystic Moon
Riding in your bed so high.
In my dreams I'll touch your face.
On spirit wings, you'll see me fly.

OH MY SISTERS

Oh my Sisters.
For we are not of the meek and obedient.
We are not of the quiet and acquiesced.
Silently raised breeders and cooks.

Oh my Sisters.
We are the wild eyed warriors.
Mother's by choice, providers by design.
We are strong barefoot Comtessa's in an Urban Jungle.
We are loud, real and ready.

Oh my Sister's.
Throw your arm's wide, and raise that primal note.
For we are The Women.

Stephanie J. Bardy

PERSEPHONE'S HEART

She pauses at the door, hand on the latch.
It is time.
She has made this trip before.
But still, she pauses, hand on the latch.

The smallest of tugs, deep in her chest.
Turns her back towards the inside.
Where he sits. Brooding into his drink.
Shadowed by the flicker of the fire.

His rugged appearance is softened in the muted light.
As he stoically refuses to look to her.
Brutal hands, that hold a world of souls,
Have been gentle upon her face.

A voice that could bring down all the mountains in the world.
Has whispered softly in her ear.
Laughed with her.
Loved with her.

She fingers the small locket at her throat.
Running her fingers over the smooth surface.
Gently shaking the 6 pieces of her fate that lay inside.
And she smiles.

On silent feet, she steals towards him.
She knows he feels her near.
The faintest of touch, just a whisper.
She kisses his cheek.

His muscles twitch and she knows.
He smiled.
She has grown to love this man.

Musings From Me

Her captor.

Again, she heads for the door.
Her heart light with anticipation of her visit.
For this is her home now.
Here she will return.

Stephanie J. Bardy

PRIMAL

Her eyes slowly close as sweat beads down her chest.
His hands softly caress her trembling thighs.
Her mouth opens slowly, to taste his passion.
The animal hungers for only lust that will quench.
Primal instinct overrides rational thought.
All breath escapes her as he tastes her love.
Reaching into her very core he shatters her harshly guarded control.
The wolf cries out only to be silenced from the pressure within.
Her back arches, her body trembles, and the hunger, the primal need, consumes them both.
Her slides slowly into her wet heat, driving all sanity and control away.

ROADS

I've walked along this dusty road, for more than half your life.
I've seen the new, I've seen the old,
I've argued wrong and right.

But never in my travels have I seen a sight like you.
Bent and twisted all around,
Your soul is split in two.

They preach to you about a love,
That batters you inside.
You closed your eyes and closed your mind and never realized.
The truth behind those gilded words,
Were silver-coated lies.

The love you seek, the peace you need, is waiting right outside.

The touch of faith, is the warm embrace of the beauty all around.
The words you pray, will always stay, like grass upon the ground.
So plant your feet, raise up your eyes, and open up your mind.
For love s all around you, in the Mother and our kind.

She'll take your hand, in the Summerland
When your crossing time has come.
She'll be that quiet voice inside,
When the questions are all done.
The wind will blow, and you will know,
She's been there all the time.
Waiting on the moment when you opened up your mind.

So when you've walked this dusty road, for more than half your life.
You've seen the old, and seen the new,
Understanding wrong from right.
I hope you find, a closed up mind, and share what you have known.

With the Gods above, and the Mother's love, share what you've been shown.
Shine a light, open sight, to the Magick that has grown.

Musings From Me

SADNESS

I have been the shoulder, the hand to hold.
I've been the smile, the heartaches told.
I've been the keeper of secrets dear,
Silent guardian of the broken tear.

The target when the anger flows.
Willingly accepting the verbal blows.
I've soaked it in and let it be.
Knowing it was frustration that needed me.

I've been turned away and pushed aside.
And been there waiting after the ride.
I've said I'm sorrys, and forgive mes too.
When I'm not sure, what else to do.

But hidden away, in my secret place.
A broken heart sits in its place.
A little tattered and worn with time.
It's all I have, and it's all mine.

Sadness sits, and waits for me.
Rolling his hands and grinning with glee.
For every so often, when the night does call
Sadness swoops in, and the tears do fall.

And the hand that I hold, in the silence at home.
Is mine and it wipes my tears all alone.
The shoulder that bears the heartaches untold.
Shake as the Sadness begins to unfold.

I weep, and I keen, and feel lost inside.
In the darkness and Sadness I've no where to hide.
But in the rays of the sun, as it raises his head.

Stephanie J. Bardy

I find comfort and solace, and push back the dread.

Just once in a while, when it gets all to much.
I need the shoulder, the hand, a comforting touch.
Someone to say, I'm here for you, I've got your back.
But really its just a Sadness attack.

I'll get through it, to another day.
And smile and be there when you say "Hey"
And give the shoulder and the hand to hold.
And hold your secrets, and heartaches untold.

Musings From Me

SCREAM

Before this came into being, I was feeling angry, frustrated, wanted to shout from the rooftops, and shake every whiny, woe is me woman, that I could find. This is the first time a poetic inspiration has come with such a strong emotion. Now that it is out, I feel calm, and more myself. This is what came from all that.

I am strong.
I can not be torn apart, beaten down, shattered, by your words.
I will not lose my footing, my knee's will not touch the earth.
I am strong and I will NOT go down.

I choose.
I see your words, your anger, out there.
Where it belongs. It does not touch me.
It is my choice what I allow in, what I allow to affect me.
I choose how I will react.

Being woman does not mean you can tear me down.
It does not mean I will get back up.
It means I will stand tall and remain firm on my feet.
Being woman, any piece that is ripped away, is a lesson learned.
And I move on.

I am Strong, I am in control of my reactions, my emotions and my environment.
I am here. Present in my body, safe in my Spirituality, and what does not nourish that, does not exist in my world.

I do not lead, I will not follow.
I will travel my road, and welcome those kindred spirits, along the way.

Stephanie J. Bardy

I stand alone, but am not alone.
For what I do not find in me, I will not find without me.

SECRET PLACES

Secret places,
And hidden dreams.
Gathered deep within my soul.
Stirring to life, they have begun,
With desire, they spring with glee.
Responding to an ancient call,
Spoken in words, in part from thee
Those secret places,
The hidden dreams,
All vying to be heard
The rush of you, within my blood
The answer to my call
How bitter sweet it is to love
When love can't have it all
My hidden places, and secret dreams
To you I offer free
For you have broken down a wall
Which long has hidden me.

Stephanie J. Bardy

SENSES AND ELEMENTS

I wrote this one a while ago, but felt I wanted to share it again. It has been a long hard winter, and inspiration has been few and far between. I am now actively pursuing my Muse. Muse had better watch out!! I thank each and every one of you for hanging in with me, and not leaving the group just yet...or thank you for being forgetful!!! LMAO!!

The sound.
The melting dripping symphony of a cold blanket turned to a running river.
The smell.
The fresh, earthy aroma of the snow soaked ground.
The feel.
The warmth of the sun, resting gently on my upturned face.
The touch.
Connecting with each vibration of life just below the surface, ready to explode.
The sight.
The tree's, gently waving their arms, in the fragrant breeze, as if to catch the attention of the Mother.
The Spirit.
The uplifting swell in my chest, as I watch the melting snow wash away the mistakes and fears of a long hard winter.
The joy.
Knowing, just as Nature is given the chance to begin again each Spring, I am too.

SHADOW DANCER

I sit in the quiet of my mind
Still and breathless
With your light dancing through me
Flashes of color dazzle my eyes
As I try to cat a glimpse
Of your face
I know your touch
Your scent
Your power
It is woven into the fabric of my slumber
Shadows danced
And a glimpse is all I am awarded
Familiar, warm
Almost known
Eluding me once more

SHINING BRIGHT
Dedicated to my Dad

As I travel through the labyrinth of life
Many a broken path I will find
Life's hard lessons
Plunged into the very heart of my core

Helpless, hopeless, drowning in a river of tears
The vines of despair weighing down my pride
I hear the distant laughter of a malicious heart
And I try and hide myself away
Shining bright and pure
There is a light
A welcome hand to help me through
It is your spirit
Your soul
I hang on to
It is your strength
That will guide me home
Ravaged body small and frail
Sleep claims you often
But your spirit shines bright
And it bathes me in love
I will hold strong to your light
And it will carry me
Through the tears
Through the pain
When your body finally lets go
I will keep the memory of you
Deep within my love
Forever will your spirit shine bright and soar
As it could not
Harnessed by the earth
Your strength

Musings From Me

Your love
Your quiet ways
Will carry on
In the smile
Of your blood line
You will become legend
To those who love you
My hero
My heart
My Father

Stephanie J. Bardy

SILENT GOODBYE

You fly now, on the wings of silence
Your once pain twisted body, released in gentle repose
Be it known you are loved by many
Be in known you are missed

Rest now valiant warrior, your battles here are through
Find your sunshine,
Find your peace,
Find your home among the stars,

Young though you were, forever young you will be,
No more disease will steal your beauty,
No more death will steal your shine,
I bid you a silent goodbye, until we cross again

SILVER LADY

Silver Lady riding high
See my face and hear my cry
Bless the ones
We cannot see
Hold the weak and set them free
Silver Lady shining bright
Know m heart with loving light
Dance across the midnight sky
In my dreams
With you, I'll fly
Silver Lady, Goddess fair
Sitting on our gilded mare
Keep your children
Safe and warm
Within your arms
And free from harm

Stephanie J. Bardy

SLEEPING GIANT

Another back deck inspiration. This one brought to you by the very large, very loved Maple Tree in my backyard.

The last of the leaves, cling valiantly to her branches.
Like defeated soldiers, bravely making their final stand.
Once vibrant colors, now muted, wave against the dull inky depths of the rain heavy clouds.

What once cradled life, sheltered many from storms, now lay bare.
Stripped of her majestic cloak, her arms reach for the sky, bereft and alone.
Abandoned by those who found a home in her. Deserted by those who sought guidance from her.

She stands. Tall and proud, quiet in her grieving. Waiting.
Waiting for the return of her love.
Waiting for the day that her body runs warm, and her fingers caress the gentle face of the Spring time air.

Her shroud will come. Blazing white and bitter cold. A blanket of forgetfulness to those who will see her.
Her beauty will hide, deep within her soul, within her roots. And she will sleep.
She will vanish into her dreams, leaving but a shell behind.

Then, when the warm breezes come to kiss her awake, she will breath.
Slowly, shyly, she will blossom to the hand of her mate.
Once again her arms will cradle the life around her, and she will be garbed in the brilliant green of her cloak.

Her beauty, hidden away for so long, will burst forth, and again she will feel love.
But for those that have known her, for those who have sat at her feet,

Musings From Me

For those who have listened to her song, they will remember.

They will remember the grace of her once barren arms.
They will remember her lessons. They will remember her proud quiet voice.
That can only be heard when the wind dances around her body so bare.

And they will wait. They will wait with her for the return of the Sun.
They will watch over her, and they will greet her each day.
So that she may know, even as she sleeps, she is loved.

Stephanie J. Bardy

SMALL THINGS

Big grand gestures,
Huge shows of thanks,
It's the small things I love,
The small things I see.

Buy me a car,
Give me a ring.
Hold my hand,
Kiss my cheek.
The small things will get my love.

Never forget the small things.
For they make up a lifetime of love.
A mental scrapbook of memories.

And last longer than any grand gesture ever could.

SOLSTICE

The darkest nights
The longest nights
Seem to never end.
The darkest times
The hardest times
Seem to never end.
But as the night is broken by the dawn.
So shall the darkest times.
The longest struggles, ended by Hope.
The hardest times, ended by Love.
As the sun rises
From your darkest, longest night
Greet the new day with Hope.
Face it with Love.
For without the our Darkness
We can never stand strong within our Light

Stephanie J. Bardy

SOME SAY

Some say, to lift your heart will make your burdens seem smaller than they are.
Some say, to force a smile will lift your spirits higher than they are.
Some say, its always worse for someone else.
Some say, just stop thinking of yourself.

But I say, my heart is to heavy to carry on my own.
But I say, my spirit has yet to find a home.
But I say, its not them who face my pain.
But I say, its not their life that starting to fade.

Some say, do for others before you take things for yourself.
Some say, take your insecurities and put them on a shelf.
Some say, each day is a gift and not a guarantee.
Some say, look beyond your own backdoor and you will see.

But I say, I need others to get me through the day.
But I say, my fear just won't go away.
But I say, I need more time, more days, for you and me.
But I say, who's there looking back for me?

Each day I fight, each day I pray.
Each smile I force brightens someone else's day.
Little by little, I am starting to fade
Lying in a bed, that I never made.

I will smile and fight,
Face each moment with forced laughter and light,
Battle this burden, weighing heavy down on me.
And just hope, that in this darkness, I will see

SOMETHING IS STIRRING

Something is stirring.
Can you feel it?
That tickle in the pit of your stomach.
The breathless anticipation of an unasked question.
Something is moving.
Can you sense it?
That shift in awareness, putting senses on alert.
The swiftly pounding heart that drums out a warning.
Something is stirring. Something is moving.
Are you ready? Are you aware? Do you know?
Breath, reach, ground, and breath. Be ready. For it comes for us all.
(inspired by a conversation...as usual)

Stephanie J. Bardy

SPRING

The pale light of dawn
Starts to brighten the sky
One, Two, Three
There are snowflakes fluttering by
"No Spring for six weeks"
The rodent said
To our dread
"Catch you all later, I'm back to bed"
So, I stand on my porch
Wishful thinking at best
Hoping for Spring
To give my shivering a rest
The birds are all quiet
As the snow continues on
Only fools are up
Before birds
In the false light of dawn
Plotting and scheming
Of what I will do
If I catch that damn rodent
I think I'll make stew
I heave a sad sigh
And go back inside
Six more weeks of this crap?
I think will hide

SPRING MOON

I am going to lay beneath the fullness of the Springtime Moon
Nestled on a bed of clover
I am going to flick my fingers and toes
Imagining fairy dust falling all around me
For I am light, for I am air,
For I am but a thought, a whisper, a dream.
For I can not be held by the trappings of my humanity.
For within my mind, I can fly.
I am going to lay beneath the fullness of the Springtime Moon
For I am all, contained within everything.

Stephanie J. Bardy

SQUIRREL, CROW AND A TREE

A Squirrel and a Crow sat on a branch, squawking as loud as can be.
"Be gone from my home" chattered the Squirrel from his spot.
"Please take yourself out of my tree. "
"I have made this my nest, for many a year.
My hole is right there, you can see.
I have gathered the nuts, the leaves I have laid, to make this a suitable tree.
So, might I suggest, and don't think I jest, that you gather yourself, and you flee."
The Crow watched the Squirrel as he flitted and fluffed.
Until his fur made him twice his real size.
He then spread his great wings, gave a fluff of his own, and settled his feathers at his side.
"Let it be know, I do not travel alone, and my companions are less understanding.
We have watched from the skies, and know your words are all lies, for we've seen the day you arrived.
So small and so weak, with barely a squeak, we are surprised that you're still alive.
So heed my words well.
Find others to tell, and scamper away with your life.
Put up not a fight, and you'll be alright, and not have to face all this strife."
As Crow settled back on his branch in the tree,
And Squirrel pondered all he'd been told.
The Great Tree gave a shake, a shudder, a groan.
For she was one of The Old.
"Now listen to me" came a voice from the Tree, soft as a breeze in the Spring.
"My branches have held your ancestor's well, protected them from oncoming storms.
They have recorded the tales, of battles that swelled between both of your feuding kind.

84

Musings From Me

They sheltered and shaded, and watched life as it faded, but it's best that you keep this in mind.
For I am the Tree, and as you can see, your fate is mine for deciding.
You must live in peace, in these branches you see, or another home you'll be finding.
We all look so different, with two legs or four, but feather's or fur do not matter.
There is enough space, in this sacred place, for all to live together.
If you love one another, like your own brother, and we all care for this ground which we stand.
Then harmony will spread, like a fire in the head, and bring peace to this battle torn land."
The Tree then fell silent, no leaf gave a rustle.
And the Squirrel and the Crow, gave any sound they could muster.
"If you gather straw" said Squirrel, with great awe.
"And I search the ground for some moss.
Two homes we could build, in these branches so still, and prevent what Tree said about loss."
Crow bowed his head, because after all that Tree said, he knew that he was no better.
For there to be peace, Ego must be released, and all must work for it together.

Stephanie J. Bardy

STALEMATE

I want to run barefoot, through a field of green.
Head thrown back, with the glee of a child.

I want to dip my toes into the brook,
As it babbles its laughing song.

I want to chain a wreath of Daisies,
To crown my sun kissed brow.

I want to spin.
Spin and spin and spin.
Watching the kaleidoscope of colors,
As they fly past my eyes, dancing with the clouds.

Grown Woman says hurry, no time for play.
Child Within, stamps her little foot and pouts.

Stalemate.

I want to work in my garden,
And wrap up in sheets off the line.

I want to create divinity for dinner,
With soup and a few lonesome potatoes.

I want to nurture my children.
Teach them lessons for life.

I want to dance with my soul mate,
Dance, and dance and dance.
Watching the reality of life,
As it flies past my eyes, faster than light.

Musings From Me

Child Within says, play, no time for work.
Grown Woman sets her hands on hips, and glares.

Stalemate.

Spirit steps forth, taking both by the hand.
She helps Grown Woman plant the Daisies,
Which grow into the crown for Child Within.
She skips with the Child Within,
As the sheets flap in the breeze of the field of green.
She teaches Grown Woman to create divinity in dinner,
Together with Child Within.

To be Grown Woman, you must have the carefree Child Within.
To be Child Within you must have the responsibility of Grown
Woman.
To be both, you must have Spirit.

Stephanie J. Bardy

SUN SHINE ON ME

Ok, so the story behind this is...I heard this one line in a commercial.
It was the only line from the song that stuck out, and my mind, such
that it is, took that line, and this is what I got.

Sun shine on me in the valley,
Sun shine on me through the clouds,
Sun shine on me, As I reap just what I've sown,
Sun shine on me all around.

And when the darker days come to hang upon my soul.
When kind words don't make a sound.
Open up my heart, and let the sun shine from within,
Plant my feet firmly on the ground.

Sun shine on me, in those places that I hide,
Sun shine on me when I'm down.
Sun shine on me dry the tears upon my cheek,
Sun shine on me when I'm loud.

And if I have to go to the darkness.
If I have to go to the ground,
Let me be the sunshine that shines on those I love,
Let me be the sunshine all around.

Sun shine on me in the valley,
Sun shine on me through the clouds.
Sun shine on me as I reap just what I've sown,
Sun shine on me all around.

SURVIVAL

What do you do, when you are suddenly so overwhelmed that you can't hold back the tears?
Where do you turn, when you have always been the one with smiles?
Who is there, to hold your hand?

How do you pick up the pieces from something you didn't even know was broken?
Where do you start moving on, when you don't know where it finished?
Where are the answers, when the questions seem so distant?

Answers never come easy, not when it counts.
Hands are few and far between when its pain that holds them.
Sometimes the smiles crack, waver, and fall, just a little.

Life only throws at you, what you can survive.
Or so they say.
Cry, when the crying is needed, laugh, even when alone.
Scream if its building to burst, but live, live in all the colors of you.

Don't shut your feelings away in a box, to be opened "someday".
Ride every roller coaster, revel in every high, every low, and all the ground in between.

To live, is to survive, to survive is to live.
So, survive, with every ounce of emotion, every tear, every step.

Live your survival in blazing colors, in true honest emotion.

Cry, when you need to, laugh when you want to, and dance in the rain, every chance you get.

Stephanie J. Bardy

THAT SILLY LITTLE BIRD

Each year I cross my fingers
My breath bated in my chest.
For that silly little bird,
With the bright red chest.

The snow may melt away.
Puddles fading in the ground.
But, each year I sit and wait.
For that bird to come around.

The tree's may weep their sap.
Bulbs may poke their heads out bold.
But that silly little bird.
Means the end to all the cold.

So, out I went today.
In my coat so thick and warm.
Out trudging in the snow.
Which has become the norm.

Much to my delight.
With wings so open wide.
That silly little bird.
Came resting at my side.

Hello there Mister Robin.
So glad to see you near.
For truly now I can say.
Spring is finally here.

THE COUNCIL

Weaving, twisting, winding, words that spin about in my head.
Plucking at the well-hidden insecurities.
"Let's draw this one out into the light!" says the voice of the head of
The Council.
Doubt.
It has chosen Doubt to be the theme for the day.
Weaving, twisting, winding those words.
Spinning them about in my head.
Courage takes a stand.
Confidence holds its hand.
"We are stronger than Doubt."
Faith joins the two and The Council is quiet.
Weaving, twisting, winding words that spin about my head.

Stephanie J. Bardy

THE DYING TIME

They call this the Dying Time
When Life goes to sleep
The coldness creeps in.
Our harvest we reap.
But I stand in a circle
Of dry cracking leaves
As I feel the night time
Tug on my sleeve.
My feet on the earth
My heart starts to pound
For what completely surrounds me
Is nothing but sound.
Life is still moving
In the dark cold and bleak
With passion and vibrance
Not silent and weak
The trees drop a shelter
For Life in the cold
And life keeps on going
Proud and so bold.
They call this the Dying Time
When Life goes to sleep
But Life just keeps changing
New places they keep.
While many may quiet
In the still of the time
Life keeps on marching
It holds its own rhyme.

Musings From Me

THE JOURNEY

There was a moment, on our way home, when three incredible, goosebumps raising, events occurred. Out of that, came this...thank you Muse.
Dedicated to Dana R. My Muse.

Road tripping with so many facets of your life.
The green blur out the window creating a bond between us all as the miles slip by.
Laughter, tears, songs and dancing, as we journey without you.
But always with you.
Friendships have started.
Bonds renewed.
As that blur of green flies by.
Road tripping with so many facets of your life.

Stephanie J. Bardy

THE LIGHT IS RETURNING

The snow is falling softly
As is it's way
The clouds are hiding the sun away
The dark is clinging
Wanting just one more say
But the light is returning
On this very day
Persephone is preparing
For her journey home
For in the Underworld
She did roam
Leaving Demeter
Heartbroken, alone
But she brings back the light
On her very own
Six months in the light
Six months in the dark
The pomegranate seeds left their mark
But the mother is ready
To receive her lark
For the light is returning
To chase out the dark
The wheel has turned
And the days grow long
The people will dance
And sing of her song
Yule brings to an end
The sleep of her gone
And Persephone will smile
For her heart is strong
The light is returning
Let us all rejoice
Fill up the skies

Musings From Me

With our praising voice
For hilltops and valleys
Of green be our choice
Let Persephone know
From even the smallest of voice
The light and the dark
Are inside of us all
The battles we wage
The leaps and the falls
But remember the light
In the harshest of squalls
For in the darkest of dark
In your heart you recall

Stephanie J. Bardy

THE MOTHER BREATHES

The snow melts.
Drip, drip, drip.
Pools of hope form as the warm rays of the sun melt away the
memory of the cold.

I have taken this time to walk. Out into the trees, still barren, but
humming with waiting life.
I walk with no particular direction in mind, and I wander deep into
the waiting arms of the forest.
I am day dreaming, living small lives within my own imagination.

I see the long shadows that are stretching towards me and I see Suna
dip her head below the gnarled fingers of the trees.

I have lost my way and wandered to far to hear anything but the life
around me.

My heart quickens, as do my steps, carrying me further and further,
until, gasping, shaking, I emerge on the edge of a small clearing.

Perfectly formed, as if some human hand had drawn the landscape. A
circle of grass, brown, lifeless, within a perfect circle of trees, each one
touching the other, so close it was hard to tell where one stopped and
the other began.

I felt something here, something special, not meant for a mere mortal
as myself, so I slide back behind the ring, and closed my eyes, to catch
my breath.

As I opened my eyes, hoping I had somehow been brought back to
the road where I had entered, I was dismayed to find I was still
staring at the ring.

Musings From Me

Somehow it had changed. Each blade of grass seemed to stretch and vibrate, almost dancing in some invisible breeze. The trees seemed to sway just beyond my vision, glimmering, shifting, breathing.

Then I see. The light, small, faint, but growing, emerging from the trees. As I watch, silent, barely breathing, fearing I would stop it, I see more lights, varying in size, color, and shape, start to emerge all around the circle.

They are women, beautiful, each in their own way. Each different, and I know their names. Not from study, not from lessons taught, but a primal, universal knowledge.

Brigit is the first to step forward fully from the trees. The flame above her brow dancing, and softly glowing about her face. She smiles and turns to the Lady next to her. Reaching out her hand, their fingers entwine together, and it goes around the circle.

Lada, Persephone, Flora.

Beiwe, Freya, Hare Ke,

Each grasping the hand of the next, each sharing their light with the other, each becoming part of something more.

Anna Perenna, Blodewedd and Dziewanna, complete the circle, and I can feel Mother take a breath.

Within the circle a woman appears. Eostra spreads her arms to the sky, and exhales.

Within that one moment the earth stood still, then she sighed. Life has returned, light has returned, and the Mother is rejoicing.

As I watch in awe, humbled by what I was permitted to witness, I see Eostra change, as each woman takes her place within the circle, not anyone more important, more honored, than the one before. Each one equal, each one an important part of the whole.

As the last faded from the center, the circle was one once more. Together they raised their arms, hand still joined, to the sky, one by one, their heads fell back, and together they welcomed Mother back from her long slumber.

Then one by one, they faded back into the shadows.

And I was alone in the circle once more. I stood for a long time in the melting snow. And I thought. I thought about the Ladies, I thought about Mother Earth, and I thought about me.

I turned to find my way back, and after a few steps, the trees opened and there was the road.

I may have stumbled upon the circle by accident, or I may have not. But as I made my way back, I knew I had been touched by something magickal. The names may vary, the paths may be different, but together they all welcomed back life, they all rejoiced with the Mother.

THE ROSE

White light presses down,
Black night creeps back into the shadows.
I take a breath, as I open my eyes.
Morning, I live once more.
Sunlight sustains me.
Warmth gives me life.
Faces pass me, fingers brush my face.
I am reborn.
Energy courses through me,
I open my mouth and scream to the heavens.
I am revitalized.
The sun begins to wane, life starts to fade from me.
Darkness creeps along the ground.
Like a silent predator, coming to claim me.
I shudder, as my last breath whispers from my lips.
I wrap my soul around myself in protection,
And the dark pushes me down.
Its clinging hands travel over my body.
As it claims me once more.
Until the sun rises, and I live.

Stephanie J. Bardy

THE VEIL

Darkness crawls across the land.
A thousand screams are whispered through the tree's,
On the breath of a windless night.

Can you hear me? The veil is thinning.
Can you see me? The veil is thinning.

Shadows dance where light dare's to tread.
Grasping hands, reaching, stretching.
Holding out for love to touch back.

Can you feel me? The veil is thinning.
Can you touch me? The veil is thinning.

Living walk among the dead.
With their sightless eyes, and soundless ears.
If they would only stop, be still, be silent.

They could hear, they could see, they could feel and touch.
For the veil is thinning, and there are messages to send.
There are lessons to receive.

For the veil is thinning.

THE WOLF

Silent tears held captive by an iron will.
Locked inside a prison of pain.
Green caresses brown, sparking to gold.
Shuttered windows to a darkened soul.
Light shimmers, tearing at the walls.
The Wolf is weakened, her will, shaken.
The tears are free for only a moment.
And she is vulnerable.
He feels nothing but the whisper of her, the slight quiver of her body
and he knows.
He has broken into her.
He has touched her where only his heart can see.

THUNDERING IDEAS AND RAMBLING ADVENTURES

You came in thundering
All big plans and grand idea's
You stormed in rambling
All adventure and promise
Then the noise calmed
The thundering stopped
And a silence enveloped me like a cold misty blanket
I walked out to find you
Curled beside the river of despair
And I sat with you
Until you came back
All thundering idea's and rambling adventure

TO TOUCH THE GODS

Fingers touch, lightly
Trembling, excited.
Lips caress flesh.
Tongue tasting, teasing, probing.

Breath soft as silk,
washes over slick wet skin.
Heartbeats match the pace.
Building, faster, stronger, harder.

Motions become frantic.
Bodies grasping, clinging, pulsating.
Riding each wave, racing higher and higher.

Screams erupt as they are shattered.
Soaring among the stars.
Bodies vibrate, and become pure sensation.

As they become one, they Touch the Gods.

Drifting, floating, like a feather,
falling to earth.

They become whole,
They become solid,
They become Two.

Fingers touch lightly.
Trembling sated.

Stephanie J. Bardy

TOUCH ME

Touch me where only our heart can see.
Look into the hazel eyes of a battered soul.
Find the pieces the remnants of me.
Call my name, feel the power to make me whole.
Touch me where only our heart can see.

UNITY

Goddess shining from our eyes
Arms raised up toward the skies
Bodies moving to the beat
Rhythms pounded from our feet
Hail to all who gather here
Welcome all and have no fear
We have come with one desire
To play our drums and dance the fire
Join us and you will see
We are all here in Unity

Stephanie J. Bardy

VOICES

Voices are screaming in my head
I ignore them
Push them back
Shut them away
They get louder
Screaming in my head
Voices are screaming in my heart
I dance
Sing and play
They get louder
Those voices screaming in my heart
My voice is screaming from my soul
Silent sound that escapes my eyes
Trails of salty wails
Whisper down my cheek
My voice screaming from my soul
I answer those voices in head
I comfort those voices in my heart
I nurture the voices in my soul
But only for awhile
Then they come back
Screaming

WARRIOR WOMAN

I am Woman
Strong, proud, determined
I have been abused, defiled
Recycled and denied
But I remain strong
I am Woman
My Power is within
I am Warrior
Strong, proud and determined
My Sword is m will
My Shield is my power
I will fight for my beliefs
I will fight though I may stand alone
I will Fight
I am Woman
I am Warrior

Stephanie J. Bardy

WHEN HE COMES

I wrote this about a month or so ago, it was late, I couldn't sleep, and
this is what came of that. It came for my Mom, so I sent it to her in an
email. I have included the email with the poem as I feel it belongs
together. I hope you enjoy.

It's 2 am and I can't sleep. Which is not unusual for me. I have to
work in the morning, so I came downstairs to have one more cigarette
before I try sleep again. As I stood on my back deck, the wind
howling louder than I have ever heard it, what I believe to be your
God, spoke to me, with these words. This is for you, you may share it
if you want, but these words came for you. I know our paths are
different, but if you can feel the spirit through my Gods, then I believe
that I can hear the words of yours. Here are those words.

When He comes,
The storms that rage upon the sea's will silence.
When He comes,
The winds will rest upon the shore.
When He comes,
There will be peace down in the valley.
When He comes, I will be afraid no more.

For when He comes,
I will stand tall for the battle.
For when He comes,
My shackles he sets free.
For when He comes,
My heart will know His glory,
And when He comes,
I know He will come and rescue me.

I will stand high upon His mountain,
I will stand strong within His mighty sea,

Musings From Me

I will stand firm, behind his shining radiance
I will stand proud, for He is all I need.

When He comes, there will be peace upon the valley.
When He comes, there will be peace for all the sea's.
When He comes, there will be peace within the anger.
For when He comes, He comes for all to see.

And with that, I now find myself very very tired. Love you Mom,
and good night. :)

Stephanie J. Bardy

WHEN THE NIGHT CLOSES IN

As still as the beat of a love long since past.
As dark as the hardest fought night.
As silent as the whisper of a put away child.
As calm as a sea before storming.

When the night closes in, there is but a moment.
A blink, a mere second of time.
When it seems as if life holds its breath as is waiting.
It's then that I feel most alive.

The sound creeps back in, with crickets and rustling.
The light finds is surface reflection.
The call of the Night Bird echoes quite loudly.
And the tree's sway gently in time.

My bones grow more weary, and rest starts its calling.
And the moment is gone in a flash.
To remain just a memory, burned into my mind.
Till the next time the night closes in.

WHERE DO YOU FIND

Where do you find the peace?
When your heart is full of storms.

Doubt clouds your every thought.
And pain your only friend.

Where do you find the comfort?
In the silence of your mind.

Screams claw at your voice.
And control just a well worn illusion.

Where do you hear the joy?
When the trees no longer sigh.

The oceans turn back,
and the rain falls, even in the sun?

You find the peace in the smile of yourself,
And the Goddess in your eyes.

You find comfort in a soft sweater.
That hugs you like a childhood memory.

You find the joy in the tiny hand of your child.
The gentle touch of your mate,
And a hot cup of tea.

You find all that you seek, is in the truth within your soul.

WOMAN AND MOTHER
A Bath

A bath.

That almost sacred time, when you slip beneath the heat of the water.

When you feel it start to creep into your bones, at the most frozen parts first.

The toes.

You slide down until only your face is above the water, and your body does that involuntary shudder as it adjusts to the almost overwhelming warmth.

All sound slips away, leaving only the beating of your heart.

Woman lives for these moments. Mother longs for them.

Woman was smart this time. She planned.

Mother hides a snicker behind her hand.

Woman made sure. Husband at work. Boy and Girl home and busy.

It was her time.

Mother hides another snicker.

The steam beckons and Woman slips in with a sigh.

Mother closes her eyes, she knows.

Woman feels her hair swirl around her as she gets deeper into the water.

Mother waits.

Woman hears nothing but her heartbeat, feels nothing but the warmth. Stress slowly starts to seep out as the heat seeps in.

She can't hear the dog sniffing under the door.

She can't hear the incessant wail of Girls music down the hall, or the droning voice coming from Boy's room.

Nothing but her heartbeat.

Mother still waits.

Then it comes.

That brutal interruption.

The knock on the door.

Woman snarls..."Busy!"

Mother tempers it with..."Sweetie"

Musings From Me

A voice. From the other side of the door.
It dares to speak.
"Mom?"
Again, Woman snarls..."I said BUSY!"
Again, Mother tempers it with "Honey."
The padding of feet down the hall is bliss to Woman and she sinks
into the heat again.
Mother waits, feeling sorry for Woman. She knows better.
The knock comes again.
"Mom?"
The Woman is spewing profanities. Mother pats her shoulder and
answers..."Yes?"
"Mom I need to ask you something."
Woman is gnashing her teeth now.
Mother replies..."Can it wait 5 minutes?"
The voice..."Not really."
Mother sighs..."Be right out."
Woman is speechless. Right. OUT?
Again, Mother pats her on the shoulder.
Hair gets washed, body gets rinsed, and all that blissful heat swirls its
way down the drain.
Woman is beyond consoling.
The knock..again..."Mom?"
Before Mother can stop her, Woman whips the door open.
Eyes blazing, hair a dripping mess stuck to her face, towel wrapped
and clutched in fingers that are turning white with tension.
Woman meets eyes of Girl.
"WHAT?"
Mother tempers that with..."Sweetheart."
That voice, the one beyond the door, now in Girl's body, meets
Woman's eyes.
Cocks an eyebrow and asks...
"What's for dinner?"

Stephanie J. Bardy

ABOUT THE POET

Stephanie Bardy, who also is known publicly as, and writes under the alias Lupa Bardy, is a fiction writer and poet of thirty plus years and looks for World domination through the written word—preferably, her words. Currently, she has multiple works presented in various publications such as books, online magazines, a local newspaper and her growing line of books.

When Stephanie's not attempting to take over the literary world, she is a mother, grandmother, lover of nature and fond user of well placed sarcasm.

www.ingramcontent.com/pod-product-compliance
Lightning Source LLC
Chambersburg PA
CBHW071558040426
42452CB00008B/1214